STICKER ENCYCLOPEDIA

Baby Animals

About this book

HOW TO USE THIS BOOK

Read the information pages and then search for the relevant stickers at the back of the book to fill in the gaps. Use the sticker outlines and labels to help you.

There are lots of extra stickers that you can use to decorate the scenes at the back of the book. It's up to you where you put them all. The most important thing is to have lots of sticker fun!

DK | Penguin Random House

Project Editor Kritika Gupta
Editor Sophie Parkes
US Executive Editor Lori Hand
Project Art Editors Charlotte Bull, Kanika Kalra
Assistant Art Editor Simran Lakhiani
Managing Editors Penny Smith, Monica Saigal
Managing Art Editors Mabel Chan, Ivy Sengupta
DTP Designers Sachin Gupta, Nand Kishore Acharya
Project Picture Researcher Sakshi Saluja
Jacket Coordinator Issy Walsh
Jacket Designer Debangshi Basu
Production Editor Abi Maxwell
Production Controller Inderjit Bhullar
Delhi Creative Heads Glenda Fernandes, Malavika Talukder
Publishing Manager Francesca Young
Creative Director Helen Senior
Publishing Director Sarah Larter

This American Edition, 2021
First American Edition, 2011
Published in the United States by DK Publishing
1450 Broadway, Suite 801, New York, NY 10018

Copyright © 2011, 2021 Dorling Kindersley Limited
DK, a Division of Penguin Random House LLC
21 22 23 24 25 10 9 8 7 6 5 4 3 2 1
001–321020–Feb/21

All rights reserved.
Without limiting the rights under the copyright reserved above, no part of this publication may be reproduced, stored in or introduced into a retrieval system, or transmitted, in any form, or by any means (electronic, mechanical, photocopying, recording, or otherwise), without the prior written permission of the copyright owner.

Published in Great Britain by Dorling Kindersley Limited

A catalog record for this book is available from the Library of Congress.
ISBN 978-0-7440-2661-0

DK books are available at special discounts when purchased in bulk for sales promotions, premiums, fund-raising, or educational use. For details, contact: DK Publishing Special Markets, 1450 Broadway, Suite 801, New York, NY 10018
SpecialSales@dk.com

Printed and bound in China

For the curious
www.dk.com

MIX Paper from responsible sources FSC www.fsc.org FSC™ C018179

This book was made with Forest Stewardship Council ™ certified paper–one small step in DK's commitment to a sustainable future.
For more information go to www.dk.com/our-green-pledge

The publisher would like to thank the following for their kind permission to reproduce their photographs:
(Key: a-above; b-below/bottom; c-center; f-far; l-left; r-right; t-top)

1 123RF.com: Eric Isselee / isselee (c/Koala). **Alamy Stock Photo:** blickwinkel (b). **Dreamstime.com:** Maradt (c). **2 Dreamstime.com:** Dewins (cla); Isselee (cla/Macaw). **3 Alamy Stock Photo:** Gatien Hze (bl). **Dreamstime.com:** Dewins (tl, crb); Wirestock (tr); Isselee (crb/Siamese); Kwiktor (br). **4–33 Dreamstime.com:** Tetyana Ksyonz (Pattern). **6 Dreamstime.com:** Photka (cb). **6–7 Dreamstime.com:** Jennifer Bray (Background); Achmat Jappie (bc). **8–9 Dreamstime.com:** Maisyaroh Nasution (Background). **9 Dreamstime.com:** Jonmilnes (tc). **Getty Images / iStock:** LyleGregg (b). **10 Dreamstime.com:** Sergey Uryadnikov (tr). **10–11 Dreamstime.com:** Luis Fernandez (Background). **11 Dreamstime.com:** Alexan24 (tc); Photoguns (br). **12 123RF.com:** Mihtiander (cra). **Dreamstime.com:** Vladimir Seliverstov (b). **13 123RF.com:** Serg_v (bl). **Dreamstime.com:** Kieran Li (crb); Martha Marks (cla); Ihor Smishko (cra). **14–15 Dreamstime.com:** Iryna1 (Background). **16 Dreamstime.com:** Joystockphoto (clb). **16–17 Dreamstime.com:** Pokki (Background). **17 123RF.com:** Martin Damen (tr). **Dreamstime.com:** Ginger Sanders (b). **18 Alamy Stock Photo:** Travis VanDenBerg (bc). **Dreamstime.com:** Lars Christnsen (bl). **Getty Images / iStock:** vlad61 (bl/coral). **18–19 Dreamstime.com:** Allexxandar (Background); Lars Christnsen. **19 Alamy Stock Photo:** Travis VanDenBerg (br/coral reef). **Getty Images / iStock:** vlad61 (br). **20 Dreamstime.com:** Olga Popova (bl). **20–21 Dreamstime.com:** Isselee; Fabrizio Robba (Background). **21 Dorling Kindersley:** Jerry Young and Jerry Young (ca). **Dreamstime.com:** Srisakorn Wonglakorn (tl). **22–23 Dreamstime.com:** Kosmos111 (Background). **23 Alamy Stock Photo:** Arya Satya (tl). **Getty Images:** Herbert Kehrer (b). **24 Alamy Stock Photo:** Avalon / Photoshot License (crb). **Dreamstime.com:** Karin Van Ijzendoorn (clb); Jfanchin (tl, bl); Abdelmoumen Taoutaou (cra). **25 Dreamstime.com:** Agami Photo Agency (crb); Jfanchin (bc); Sergey Uryadnikov (t). **Getty Images / iStock:** Pierivb (clb). **26 Dorling Kindersley:** Neil Fletcher (clb). **Dreamstime.com:** Digoarpi (bl); Gerónimo Contreras Flores (Background). **27 Dreamstime.com:** Dewins (tc); Ekays (cra); Maxwell De Araujo Rodrigues (Background); Eric Isselee (bl). **28 Dreamstime.com:** Aleksandr Frolov (tr); Wilmy Van Ulft (Background). **29 Dreamstime.com:** Martin Brayley (Background); Lifang1025 (tr); Mikael Males (cr); Larry Metayer (br). **30 Dreamstime.com:** Biletskiy (Background); Glenn Nagel (br); Vitalii Mamchuk (bc, crb). **31 Dreamstime.com:** Andreanita (tr); James Steidl (ca, cb); Rustamank (Background). **32 Alamy Stock Photo:** Arturo de Frias (clb). **Dreamstime.com:** Grafner (Background); Pawel Przybyszewski (tr). **Getty Images / iStock:** akinshin (Bubble). **33 Dreamstime.com:** Tony Bosse (Background); Amit Rane (bl); Olgakotsareva (fbl); Tiggy7 (br). **34–35 Dreamstime.com:** Christopher Meder. **36–37 Dreamstime.com:** Cristina Bernhardsen. **38–39 Getty Images / iStock:** goinyk. **40 Getty Images / iStock:** RomoloTavani. **42 Alamy Stock Photo:** Blickwinkel (cl); Nature Picture Library (bl). **Dreamstime.com:** Eric Isselee (tr, c). **Fotolia:** Eric Isselee (fcl, cb, cb/Deer, cb/Panda, bc); Lipowski (ftl). **43 123RF.com:** Eric Isselee / isselee (fcrb); Anurak Ponapatimet (cb/puppy). **Alamy Stock Photo:** blickwinkel (bl). **Dreamstime.com:** Anankkml (tr); Jonmilnes (ca); Isselee (ca/owlet). **Fotolia:** Altenburger / arrxxx (cr); Ramona Smiers (cb). **Getty Images:** Frank Krahmer / Photographer's Choice RF (cla). **46 123RF.com:** Eric Isselee / isselee (clb); Duncan Noakes (ftl); Mihtiander (tr/coral reef); Anurak Ponapatimet (cl). **Alamy Stock Photo:** Gatien Hze (br); Edo Schmidt (c). **Dreamstime.com:** Alexan24 (cra); Bobby J Norris (tl); Andy Chia (tr); Luboslav Ivanko (cla); Photozlaja (cr); Eric Isselee (fcl); Kieran Li (cb); Mikael Males (bl); Martha Marks (bc). **Fotolia:** Eric Isselee (ca). **47 123RF.com:** Eric Isselee / isselee (ca). **Alamy Stock Photo:** Paul Fleet (bl); Michael Willis (clb). **Dorling Kindersley:** Jerry Young (crb); Booth Museum of Natural History, Brighton (cb/Ornithorhynchus anatinus). **Dreamstime.com:** Bennymarty (cla); Lianquan Yu (tc); Natalia Volkova (tr); Eric Isselee (cra); Brooke Parish (cl); Isselee (cr); Wirestock (br). **Fotolia:** Eric Isselee (cb). **50 Alamy Stock Photo:** Nature Picture Library (cl). **Dorling Kindersley:** (br). **Dreamstime.com:** 1911guy (bl); Nomadimages (tc); Sallydexter (tr); Eric Isselee (cra); Ond Èej Prosický (c); Toui2001 (crb); Lars Christnsen (crb/Aquarium fish); Peterclark1985 (bc). **Fotolia:** Eric Isselee (ca, cra/Ostrich); Ramona Smiers (cb); Lipowski (fbr). **Getty Images:** Michael Urban / DDP / AFP (ca/stork). **51 Alamy Stock Photo:** Blickwinkel (tl); Chris Mattison (clb); Juniors Bildarchiv GmbH (cr). **Dreamstime.com:** Alantunnicliffe (cra); Mirkorosenau (tr); Yuval Helfman (cla); Sarah2 (cla/toad); Lars Christnsen (cb); Srisakorn Wonglakorn (fbr). **Fotolia:** Altenburger / arrxxx (ca); Eric Isselee (fcl). **SuperStock:** Norbert Wu (crb). **54 123RF.com:** Anurak Ponapatimet (cb/puppy). **Alamy Stock Photo:** Avalon / Photoshot License (bl); Paul Fleet (cra); Arya Satya (crb/larva). **Dreamstime.com:** Agami Photo Agency (bc); Irina Kozhemyakina (tl); Roberto Okamura (tc); Andy Chia (ftr); Palex66 (tr); Natalia Volkova (cl); Dewins (c/leaf); Andy Nowack (clb); Isselee (crb, cb); Abdelmoumen Taoutaou (br). **Fotolia:** Altenburger / arrxxx (cla). **Getty Images:** Ajay Ojha (c). **55 123RF.com:** Eric Isselee / isselee (cra/bonobo, c); Duncan Noakes (bc/elephant). **Dreamstime.com:** Bennymarty (cb/wombat); Karin Van Ijzendoorn (tl); Isselee (tc, tr, ca, ca/Tortoise); Eric Isselée / Isselee (cra); Dewins (ca/leaf, cb/Leaf); Ekays (cr, bc); Vladimir Melnik (clb); Wirestock (cr/chameleon); Eric Isselee (cb/Tiger); Kwiktor (bl); Denboma (br). **Fotolia:** Eric Isselee (cla, cla/Wolf, cra/fawn, cb, c/Cub). **Getty Images / iStock:** Pierivb (cla/Giraffes). **58 Alamy Stock Photo:** Michael Willis (c). **Dorling Kindersley:** Booth Museum of Natural History, Brighton (cb). **Dreamstime.com:** Ganna Aibetova (ca/hedgehog); Amwu (tr); Eric Isselee (ca, c/Tiger, crb/Anteater); Eric Isselee / Isselee (ca/Kiwi); Aleksandr Frolov (cla); Twildlife (cra); Feng Yu (bl); Isselee (bc); Dalia Kvedaraite (bc/chick); Maradt (br). **Fotolia:** Eric Isselee (crb); Lipowski (ca/chameleon). **59 123RF.com:** Eric Isselee / isselee (cb); Anthony Lister (cl). **Alamy Stock Photo:** Nature Picture Library (cb/octopus). **Depositphotos Inc:** MennoSchaefer (c). **Dreamstime.com:** Asdf_1 (tl); Kertu Saarits (tr); Tiggy7 (ca/tadpoles); Anankkml (cra); Jonmilnes (ca/angel fish); Balagula (ca/kingfisher); Pawel Przybyszewski (bc); Greg Amptman (bc/Shark); Artushfoto (br); Cammeraydave (crb). **Fotolia:** Ramona Smiers (ca/parrots); Valeriy Kalyuzhnyy / StarJumper (ca). **62 123RF.com:** Eric Isselee / isselee (clb, bl); Thawat Tanhai (cl). **Dreamstime.com:** Balagula (tc); Natalia Volkova (tc/foal); Eric Isselee (ca, c/Tiger, cb/python); Ziga Camernik (cra); Rinus Baak / Rinusbaak (c); Isselee (br). **Fotolia:** Altenburger / arrxxx (bc); Eric Isselee (ca/fawn, fcr); Ramona Smiers (cb). **63 123RF.com:** Steve Byland / steve_byland (br); ferli (cra); Eric Isselee / isselee (crb); Christian Musat / musat (bc). **Alamy Stock Photo:** Michael Willis (cb). **Dorling Kindersley:** Liberty's Owl, Raptor and Reptile Centre, Hampshire, UK (tl). **Dreamstime.com:** Isselee (cb/Panda); Wirestock (fcrb). **Fotolia:** Lipowski (tc). **66 123RF.com:** Eric Isselee / isselee (c); Anurak Ponapatimet (tl); Duncan Noakes (fbr). **Dreamstime.com:** Amwu (bc); Eric Isselée / Isselee (tc); Vladimir Melnik (tr); Delstudio (cra); Dalia Kvedaraite (cr); Pawel Przybyszewski (bc/crab); Eric Isselee (bc/Anteater, bc/Tiger). **Fotolia:** Eric Isselee (fcr, fcrb, fbl, bl, bc/wolf, bc/fawn, bc/owlet); Lipowski (br). **Getty Images:** David Tipling / Digital Vision (cl). **67 123RF.com:** Eric Isselee / isselee (bc/Jaguar); Anurak Ponapatimet (fbr). **Alamy Stock Photo:** Paul Fleet (ca/orca). **Dorling Kindersley:** Linda Pitkin (cl). **Dreamstime.com:** Balagula (fbl); Caan2gobelow (ca); Andy Nowack (tr); Digitalbalance (cra); Pawel Przybyszewski (c, bc/crab); Isselee (fcrb, bl, br); Andy Chia (ftr, bl/parrotfish); Eric Isselee (bc, bc/foal); Wirestock (bc/kangaroo). **70 123RF.com:** ferli (7:6); Eric Isselee / isselee (3:3, 3:9); Duncan Noakes (2:1); Anurak Ponapatimet (1:4, 9:9). **Alamy Stock Photo:** Paul Fleet (5:7); Michael Willis (7:8). **Dorling Kindersley:** Booth Museum of Natural History, Brighton (8:6). **Dreamstime.com:** John Anderson (8:3, 12:8); Andy Nowack (3:7); Cammeraydave (7:2); Isselee (3:2, 5:2, 1:8, 12:9, 6:9, 9:2, 10:5, 10:8, 7:5); Natalia Volkova (1:2, 12:4); Eric Isselee (2:7, 8:1, 1:7, 10:3); Lars Christnsen (5:4); Jonmilnes (6:5, 13:1); Wirestock (10:4); Pawel Przybyszewski (6:3, 10:7); Andy Chia (2:6, 10:2); Eric Isselée / Isselee (5:1, 4:2, 11:5); Bennymarty (4:7, 13:6). **Fotolia:** Altenburger / arrxxx (8:4); Eric Isselee (4:5, 1:5, 3:8, 1:9, 5:8, 11:7); Valeriy Kalyuzhnyy / StarJumper (6:7, 12:2); Ramona Smiers (11:8); Lipowski (4:6, 12:5). **71 123RF.com:** ferli (11:6); Duncan Noakes (11:3); Anurak Ponapatimet (2:3); Eric Isselee / isselee (2:1, 12:3). **Alamy Stock Photo:** Paul Fleet (12:8); Michael Willis (11:5). **Dorling Kindersley:** Booth Museum of Natural History, Brighton (7:3). **Dreamstime.com:** John Anderson (6:5); Andy Nowack (2:4, 8:7); Eric Isselee / Isselee (4:2, 7:1); Jonmilnes (8:5); Isselee (1:6, 11:7, 2:2, 3:4, 7:5, 11:4, 13:6, 11:9, 13:9, 4:1, 2:5); Bennymarty (7:4); Wirestock (10:1); Andy Chia (4:5); Eric Isselee (9:6, 5:7, 13:1, 3:8, 8:8); Cammeraydave (6:9, 12:6); Pawel Przybyszewski (6:3, 13:8); Natalia Volkova (9:1); Balagula (2:8, 10:2); Lars Christnsen (12:5). **Fotolia:** Altenburger / arrxxx (1:8, 10:9); Valeriy Kalyuzhnyy / StarJumper (12:4); Eric Isselee (5:6, 5:5, 3:3, 12:9, 5:2, 7:2); Lipowski (6:8); Ramona Smiers (9:4)

Cover images: *Front:* **Dreamstime.com:** Isselee cb, Sonsedskaya c; **Fotolia:** Dixi crb, Eric Isselee br; **Getty Images:** Xuanyu Han (Background); **Getty Images / iStock:** Frankhuang cr; *Back:* **123RF.com:** Duncan Noakes cb; **Alamy Stock Photo:** Melba Photo Agency cb/ (Star); **Dreamstime.com:** Eric Isselee cl; **FLPA:** Thomas Marent / Minden Pictures tr; **Getty Images:** Xuanyu Han (Background); *Spine:* **Getty Images / iStock:** Frankhuang t

All other images © Dorling Kindersley
For further information see: www.dkimages.com

Contents

Looking at baby animals

Many baby animals are cute and cuddly. Some hatch out of eggs, while others are born live. Some young animals look like their parents from birth. Others begin to look like their parents as they grow up.

CYGNET

Baby swans, or cygnets, start swimming soon after birth. They swim close to their mother to stay warm and protected.

WOLF PUP

A baby wolf is called a pup. When it is born, a wolf pup cannot see or hear. It is covered with short, grayish-brown fur.

FACT!

Kittens cannot hear or see properly until they are about three weeks old.

GIRAFFE CALF

A baby giraffe, or calf, has small horns on its head and brown spots on its body. These spots help it remain hidden in the grass.

PIGLET

Piglets have four pointed toes on each foot. They use only two of these toes for walking. This means they stand on their toes like ballet dancers do.

LAMB

Baby sheep are called lambs. Most lambs can stand an hour after they are born.

5

Newborn baby animals

Just like a baby brother or sister, animal babies are small and helpless. They need to be fed, cleaned, and cared for. But some newborn animals, such as tortoises, can care for themselves from birth.

Kitten

A newborn kitten can open its eyes about a week after its birth. It cuddles close to its mother for the first three weeks of its life to keep itself warm.

Puppy

Newborn puppies sleep a lot. For about ten days after birth, they do nothing except sleep and eat.

FACT!

All kittens are born with blue eyes, which begin to change color after about a month.

Calf

A calf can stand up on its wobbly legs soon after it is born, and begins to walk the same day. The calf knows its mother by her smell.

Chick

A chick can breathe even when it is still inside the egg. When a mother hen clucks, it chirps back to her from inside.

Tiger cub

A tiger cub is born with a thick fur coat. At first, it feeds only on its mother's milk. The cub hunts with its mother after about six months.

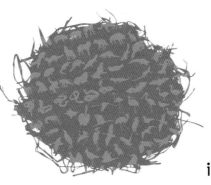

Baby mice

Newborn mice are bald, with no fur on their bodies. After a couple of days, they are covered in soft baby fuzz.

Baby tortoise

A baby tortoise breaks out of its shell using a special egg tooth, which falls off shortly after hatching.

Family life

Many baby animals live with their families. Some babies, such as walrus calves, stay with their parents until they are nearly five years old. Others take care of themselves soon after birth.

Penguins with chicks

Adult penguins feed and take care of their chicks. Sometimes they leave them with a group of other chicks while they go hunting for food.

Owl family

A male owl gathers food while the female stays in the nest with her eggs. After the eggs hatch and the owlets are older, the mother helps the father hunt for food.

Walrus and calf

If a mother walrus thinks her calf is in danger, she picks it up with her flippers, holds it close, and dives into the water.

DID YOU KNOW?

An elephant calf weighs around 250 lb (113 kg) when it is born.

Elephant family

Elephants often travel together in a line. If there is any sign of danger, the older elephants surround the babies to protect them.

Guinea pigs

Guinea pig pups go to their mother only when they need milk or want to be cuddled. They chirp loudly when they are hungry.

Angelfish

Young angelfish often live in a group and swim together in shoals for protection.

FACT!

All lion cubs are born with tawny black spots that disappear as they grow older.

Lioness with cubs

A family of lions, lionesses, and cubs is called a pride. The mothers in a pride may care for cubs that are not their own.

Playing

Just like you, baby animals love to play. Some young ones like to play with their brothers and sisters. Others love to play with toys.

Guinea pig pup

A guinea pig pup enjoys exploring and running around. It also likes to burrow and play with toys.

Bear cubs

A bear cub stands on its two legs when wrestling with other cubs. While playing, bear cubs may even bite each other gently.

DID YOU KNOW?

Bear cubs make a lot of noise while fighting, but they play very quietly.

Tiger cubs

Tiger cubs are very playful. They love to chase each other, wrestle with their paws, and play with their mother's tail.

Baby deer

Baby deer, or fawns, are fast runners. They like to race and play tag with each other. Long, thin legs allow them to jump high.

Feeding

Baby animals need to eat regularly so that they stay healthy and grow faster. Parents feed their young in different ways.

Caterpillar

Caterpillars are hungry all the time. Most of them eat leaves. A few also eat the eggs of other insects, plus aphids and ant larvae.

Flamingo chick

A flamingo feeds milk made in its throat lining to its chick. The flamingo chick feeds only on this milk when it is born.

Wolf pups

A mother wolf feeds her pups with her watery milk—this keeps them from getting sick. They begin eating meat when they are 4–5 weeks old.

FACT!

Baby birds open their beaks wide and chirp loudly when they are hungry.

Goat kid

Baby goats begin to nibble on hay and green grass when they are very young. They have eight small teeth in their lower jaw for tearing the food.

Baby animal groups

All kinds of animals live on Earth. They can be divided into five main groups. An animal may be a fish, bird, reptile, amphibian, mammal, or an invertebrate.

FISH

A parrotfish is a kind of fish. It gets its name because, when it is an adult, its teeth form a parrot-like beak. The body of a young parrotfish changes color as it grows up.

DID YOU KNOW?
Baby penguins cannot fly. They use their flippers for swimming in cold water.

BIRDS

An egret is a bird. These egret chicks have fuzzy white feathers. Egrets use their sharp bills to catch fish in water.

AMPHIBIANS

A salamander is an amphibian. This young tiger salamander is brown with dark spots that later turn to bars or irregular shapes. Many are born in water, and then move to land.

MAMMALS

A donkey is a mammal. This baby donkey (foal) has a thick, fluffy coat. Its ears are long and pointed.

INVERTEBRATES

A tarantula spider is an invertebrate. This baby sheds its skin many times a year as it grows. It can grow up to be as big as a dinner plate.

Mammals

Most baby mammals grow fur or hair on their bodies. They breathe with their lungs and feed on their mothers' milk. Most mammals give birth to live young.

Baby hippo

A baby hippo is born underwater. As soon as it is born, its mother gently pushes it to the surface to breathe.

Zebra foal

When a zebra foal is born, it is white and brown in color. The brown turns to black as the foal gets older. It takes its first steps soon after it is born.

FACT!

A quokka joey stays in its mother's pouch for about six months after its birth.

Quokka joey

A quokka joey is about the size of a raisin when it is born. It does not start looking like a quokka until it is older.

Kangaroo joey

A newborn kangaroo joey is only 1 in (2.5 cm) long. It stays in its mother's pouch for about four months before it can explore on its own.

Baby whale

When a baby whale is hungry, it bumps its mother. She then squirts thick milk into its mouth.

Baby platypus

Unlike other baby mammals, this baby hatches from an egg. It has a bill like a duck. When it is older, it uses its bill to scoop out worms from water.

Baby meerkat

A baby meerkat is born in a burrow. It feeds on its mother's milk until it starts hunting for food on its own.

Black panther cub

This cub has blackish brown fur. Mother and cub greet each other by rubbing their faces or bodies together.

Koala joey

At the time of birth, a koala joey is blind and deaf. It grows in its mother's pouch for about six months.

Baby wombat

A baby wombat is carried in its mother's pouch for about five months. Once it is out of the pouch, it starts nibbling on grass.

Baby sloth

A baby sloth holds onto its mother for about a year after being born. It cannot eat on its own and licks food from its mother's mouth.

Birds

All birds have feathers and two feet. They have a beak, but no teeth. Birds lay eggs, and chicks hatch out of these eggs. Most chicks cannot see when they are born.

Baby robin

Baby robins are born with very few feathers. But after two weeks they grow full feathers and can move their wings.

Kiwi chick

A kiwi's eggs are bigger than those of a hen. A newborn chick has a lot of fuzzy hair, which sometimes makes it look larger than its parents.

Baby stork

This young stork is learning to fly. Its beak is now black but it will start turning red when it is three months old.

Dove squab

Parent doves make a milky substance in their throats. A baby dove, or squab, pokes its beak into its parent's throat to drink it.

Baby parrot

Newborn parrots have no feathers. Later they grow green, red, or even gray feathers.

Woodpecker

A woodpecker chick is fed by its parents when young. Later, it learns how to use its sharp beak and dig holes in trees.

Ostrich chick

An ostrich chick grows inside its egg for about 40 days. It is ready to walk as soon as it hatches and leaves the nest within a day of being born.

Swallow chicks

Adult swallows feed their chicks insects rolled into a ball. They feed the chicks as many as 20 insects at a time.

Peachicks learn to feed by following their mother.

DID YOU KNOW?
Peacocks do not grow their colorful feathers until they are two years old.

Fish

All fish live in water. They breathe through their gills and swim with the help of their fins. Shiny scales cover their body.

Butterfly fish

This baby is born with sharp, pointed bones on its body. These protect it from being eaten by larger fish. The bones disappear as it grows up.

Swordfish

This young swordfish gets its name because of its swordlike bill. Once it grows up, it uses this bill to hunt its prey in the ocean waters.

Herring

Young herrings feed on small fish. The herrings take about four years to develop fully.

Catfish
After hatching, baby catfish stay in their nests for about ten days. Later, they start looking for food on their own.

Piranha
Piranhas are dangerous creatures that can eat their prey live. This young piranha eats the fins and flesh of other fish that come near it.

Koi fish
These babies can be different colors, such as silver, red, blue, or yellow. Their colored scales can take up to a year to appear.

DID YOU KNOW?
Newborn goldfish are shiny brown in color. They turn golden when they are a year old.

Young goldfish don't have a stomach to store food.

Reptiles and amphibians

Reptiles, such as snakes and lizards, have rough, scaly skin. Amphibians, such as salamanders and toads, have smooth, damp skin. Most baby reptiles and amphibians hatch from eggs. They live both on land and in water.

Baby iguana
This bright green baby iguana has sharp claws that help it climb trees. It can shed its tail to quickly get away from predators.

Baby alligator
A baby alligator is born on land. Its mother later carries it in her mouth to the water. Its flat tail helps it swim.

DID YOU KNOW?
Baby Komodo dragons grow up to become the largest lizards on Earth.

Baby salamander
This young salamander sprays a poisonous liquid from its skin to protect itself.

Komodo dragon
A baby Komodo dragon rolls in its own poop. The foul smell protects it from adult Komodos.

Gila monster

A young Gila monster feeds on the eggs of other reptiles. If they are buried underground, it uses its sharp claws to dig them up.

Baby python

When hunting, this young python wraps its slender body tightly around its prey.

Baby snakes look after themselves as soon as they hatch from eggs.

FACT!

A baby snake sheds its outer layer of skin many times as it grows.

Baby frilled lizard

This baby lizard opens up the bright orange and yellow frill around its neck to scare other animals.

Common toad

This young toad is born in water. It has a small tail that disappears when it grows into an adult.

Baby ringneck snake

A baby ringneck snake is born with a colored ring around its neck.

Invertebrates

Animals that don't have a backbone are called invertebrates. This group includes all insects. Some invertebrates, such as snails, hatch out of eggs. Others, such as baby scorpions, are born live.

DID YOU KNOW?
The wings of a butterfly are covered with tiny, colorful scales.

Baby cicada
A baby cicada, or nymph, stays underground for 13–17 years. When it finally digs its way to the surface, the nymph sheds its skin and grows into a cicada.

Baby crab
A young crab has a hard outer case covering its body. The crab replaces the case with a bigger one every time it grows.

Baby silkworm
Newborn silkworms are covered with tiny black hair. Later, they shed their skin and turn white in color.

Baby cricket
A baby cricket is born without wings. They only start growing about one month after its birth.

Baby starfish

A baby starfish is not star shaped like its parents. It develops this shape as it grows older. This young starfish now looks like its parents.

Golden tortoise beetle larva

A baby golden tortoise beetle, or larva, is flat and spiny. A growing larva eats plants.

FACT!

Baby tarantulas eat the yolk sac from which they hatch.

The first thing a baby snail does after birth is find food. It usually eats its own eggshell.

Baby sea anemone

Sea anemone babies grow attached to the bottom of the adult. They break off when they are big enough to live on their own.

Baby animal homes

Animals build nests, burrows, or dens to raise their young. Some make their homes in very cold places covered with snow. Others live in hot, sandy deserts or oceans, rivers, and lakes. Here are some of the different places where animals live.

DESERTS

Deserts are dry places with little water, so few plants grow here. Deserts are usually covered with sand or rocks. They can be hot or cold.

RIVERBANKS

A riverbank is the muddy land at the side of a river. Animals found here, such as hippos, crocodiles, and water birds, can live both on land and in water.

FORESTS

Forests are large areas where lots of trees and plants grow. Tree animals, such as squirrels, and ground animals, such as hedgehogs, live here.

GRASSLANDS

Grass, shrubs, and bushes grow in grasslands. They are home to grass-eating animals, such as giraffes and antelope, and meat eaters, such as lions and cheetahs.

POLAR REGIONS

The northernmost (Arctic) and the southernmost (Antarctic) regions are the coldest places on Earth. The sea is mostly covered with ice.

Grasslands

Grasslands are huge areas filled with grasses and varieties of trees and shrubs. They are home to herds of grazing animals. Baby animals sometimes hide in the long grass while their parents go out searching for food.

Lion cub

A lioness hides her newborn cubs in thick bushes for about six weeks. After this time, she teaches her young how to sneak up on their prey and catch it.

Baby chameleon

All chameleon babies can change color from birth. This baby has changed its color to green to hide among the leaves and catch insects.

Ferret kit

Ferret babies, known as kits, are born in dens left by prairie dogs in the grasslands. Mothers hunt small animals, such as rabbits or lizards, and bring the meat for the kits to the den.

FACT!

Fawns give out very little scent. This protects them from bigger animals in the grasslands.

Baby tortoise

Baby tortoises are land animals. They feed on grass, leaves, and flowers. Some also eat worms or insect larvae.

Rainforests

Rainforests are hot, lush forests that get a lot of rain. Here, baby animals survive in different ways. Some hide in nests on tall trees. Others simply stick close to their mothers for protection.

Baby macaw
Three-month-old macaws feed on fruit and seeds found in the rainforest. They quickly learn from their parents which fruit to pick from which tree at different times of the year.

Toucan chick
These young toucans use their large beaks to pick fruit from trees. As the chicks grow, so do their beaks.

DID YOU KNOW?
A five-week-old pygmy marmoset can climb up trees without its parents' help.

Jaguar cub
A jaguar cub can easily go into water and catch fish like its parents. Jaguars live near rivers and swamps, or in thick rainforests.

Baby chimpanzee
A baby chimp learns how to walk, climb, and eat by watching its mother. When a little older, it builds its own sleeping nest in the treetops.

Deserts

Deserts are hot, dry places with miles of sand and little water. Some young animals have fur to protect them from the hot sand. Others drink a lot of water all at once, so they don't need water for months.

DID YOU KNOW?
A baby camel opens and closes its nose to keep out sand and dust.

Desert scorpion

A baby desert scorpion uses its eight legs to crawl over rocky desert. It usually comes out at night, when it is cooler.

Sidewinder snakelet

This young snake moves by shifting its whole body sideways. This helps it move easily on the slippery desert sand.

Baby thorny devil

This baby lizard has spines all over its body—even around its eyes. When it rains, water droplets run down the spines straight into its mouth.

Roadrunner chick

These chicks are born in nests made on shrubs or clusters of cactus plants. Their long legs help them run around quickly to catch insects.

Desert locust

This young locust, or hopper, is born without wings. It walks across sandy soil.

Forests and woodlands

Forests and woodlands are home to many baby animals. Here they feed on leaves and fruit. The thick bushes and shrubs also offer many places to hide.

Quail chick
Quail chicks hatch out of their eggs in less than a month. They can leave the nest with their parents soon after hatching.

Baby hedgehog
A baby hedgehog is born with soft spines. After around 12 days from its birth, harder spines grow in their place.

Baby squirrel
A newborn squirrel has no hair or teeth for up to three weeks. Once its teeth grow fully, it chews on tree branches to sharpen them.

Raccoon kits
A baby raccoon is born with its eyes closed. Its eyes open after 20 days. It can then follow its mother in search of food.

Baby mole
A baby mole has very sharp claws. When it is older it grows thick fur all over its body, except on its pink paws and nose.

Mountains

Life can be difficult for animals living high up in the mountains. Many baby animals grow thick fur to keep warm from the cold. Some even develop strong feet to climb up cliffs.

Baby red panda
This shy baby eats solid food three months after its birth. It mainly eats bamboo shoots found in the mountains.

Baby llama
A baby llama's mother hums to it when it is born. All the female llamas in the herd surround it at birth to protect it from preying animals.

Baby yak
A baby yak has a thick, hairy coat. This protects it from the cool mountain air. At night, adult yaks huddle around the baby to keep it warm.

A snow leopard is born with a thick coat of fur. This helps it stay warm in cold, snowy mountains.

Hummingbird chick
These babies cannot fly until, at three weeks old, they grow feathers. They can then fly backward, sideways, and even hover in midair.

Polar regions

Polar regions are icy areas in the Arctic and the Antarctic. Most baby animals living here have a thick, hairy coat to protect them from the cold. Others have strong feet to walk in deep snow or white fur to hide from bigger animals.

Albatross chick

An albatross chick feeds on the fish and squid that its parents catch. Once the chick's wings grow, it flies away from its nest to live at sea.

Polar bear cub

Polar bear cubs are born blind and helpless. They stay in snow dens to keep warm.

Baby reindeer

A baby reindeer, or fawn, is born without horns. The horns grow when it is about a year old. Its thick, brown fur turns gray in winter.

FACT!

A baby reindeer can run faster than a human.

Penguin chick

The fluffy feathers on this baby's flippers become smooth and waterproof a month after birth. It can then use its flippers to swim.

Arctic fox pup

A newborn Arctic fox has brown fur. This turns white as it grows older. Its thick, padded paws help it walk on slippery ice.

Oceans

The ocean is home to different fish and other sea creatures. Most young hatch out of eggs laid at the bottom of the ocean. However, there are some that are born near the surface of the water.

FACT!

A growing crab is called a megalops, which means "big eyes."

Baby clown triggerfish

A young clown triggerfish has white spots all over its body. As it grows up, it develops leopard-like brown spots.

Baby lobster

A baby lobster has a hard shell on its body to protect it. As it grows older, it breaks out of its old shell and grows a new one.

Baby octopus

A young octopus can spray a special dark-colored ink. This colors the water around it and scares bigger animals nearby.

Shark pup

Some sharks, such as this dogfish shark, hatch out of eggs. Others, such as bull sharks, give birth to live young.

Baby blue whale

A newborn baby whale is as heavy as an adult hippopotamus. It stays with its mother for about a year after birth.

Baby lumpfish

The green color of this baby lumpfish helps it hide among underwater plants and escape bigger sea creatures.

Rivers, lakes, swamps

Baby animals that live in rivers, lakes, and swamps are either born underwater or hatch on land, and slowly make their way to the water.

Baby crocodile

A baby crocodile lies still in shallow water, waiting for prey. It leaps out in a flash and snaps up insects, frogs, fish, and other small animals.

DID YOU KNOW?

Young crocodiles are often eaten by adult crocodiles.

Dragonfly nymph

A dragonfly nymph has a pair of sharp jaws attached to its lower lip. These are folded back under its head. It shoots them out to catch water insects.

Young kingfisher

This young bird's first dive into water happens about four days after leaving its nest. The parent drops fish into water for the young one to catch.

River otter pup

If an otter pup is frightened of water, its mother gently nudges and pushes the pup toward it.

It takes 35–45 days to grow into an adult a gliding frog tadpole.

Tadpole

A tadpole's long tail helps it swim easily. Like a fish, a tadpole breathes using gills. It has no legs or arms.

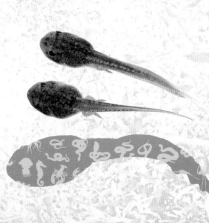

CHECKLIST

Use the stickers at the back of the book to fill this lush, green rainforest. Here are some animals that live here:

- [ ] Pygmy marmoset
- [ ] Green tree python
- [ ] Howler monkey
- [ ] Caterpillar
- [ ] Macaw
- [ ] Jaguar
- [ ] Anteater
- [ ] Toucan
- [ ] Tree frog
- [ ] Parrot

Desert

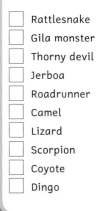

CHECKLIST

37

Use the stickers in the book to fill the desert scene. These are some of the baby animals you might find here:

- [ ] Rattlesnake
- [ ] Gila monster
- [ ] Thorny devil
- [ ] Jerboa
- [ ] Roadrunner
- [ ] Camel
- [ ] Lizard
- [ ] Scorpion
- [ ] Coyote
- [ ] Dingo

Polar

CHECKLIST

Use the stickers in this book to fill the scene. Here are some animals that live in the polar region.

- [ ] Harp seal pup
- [ ] Baby reindeer
- [ ] Penguin chick
- [ ] Polar bear cub
- [ ] Baby moose
- [ ] Albatross chick
- [ ] Arctic hare

Ocean

Use the stickers in this book to fill the ocean scene. These are some of the animals that live here. Which is your favorite?

- [ ] Seahorse
- [ ] Blue whale
- [ ] Dolphin
- [ ] Jellyfish
- [ ] Salmon
- [ ] Lobster
- [ ] Garfish